Withdrawn

**Please check all items for damages
before leaving the Library.
Thereafter you will be held
responsible for all injuries
to items beyond reasonable wear.**

Helen M. Plum Memorial Library

Lombard, Illinois

A daily fine will be charged for
overdue materials.

BOOKWORMS

GUESS WHO

Bites

Apple Jordan

mc Marshall Cavendish
Benchmark
New York

See my tongue!

I use it to taste and smell.

See my mouth!

I open it wide.

I eat my food in one
big gulp.

5

See my eyes!

They are always open—
even when I sleep.

See my body!

It is long and thin.

It can **coil** like a rope.

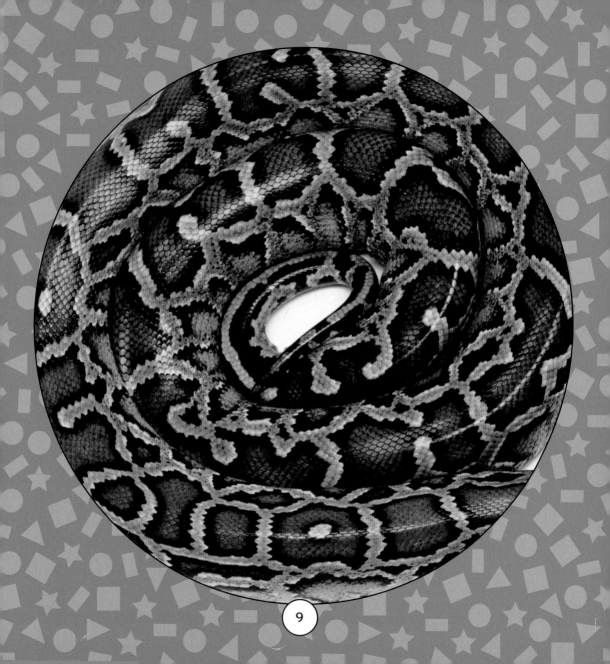

See my skin!

I **shed** my old skin.

I have new skin
underneath.

Hear me hiss!

I scare away **predators**.

See my teeth!

Watch out!

If you come too close,
I may bite.

See me move!

I **slither** away fast on my belly.

Who am I?

I am a snake!

Who Am I?

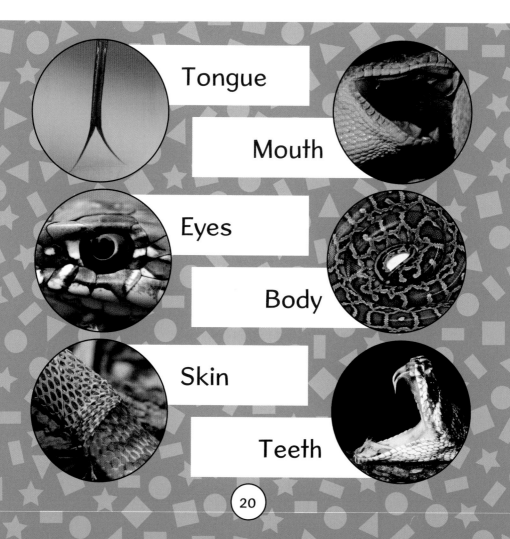

Tongue

Mouth

Eyes

Body

Skin

Teeth

Challenge Words

Coil (koil) to curl up

Shed to lose or get rid of

Slither (SLITH-er) to slide on the ground

Underneath (uhn-der-NEETH) below

Predator (PRED-uh-ter) an animal that hunts another animal

Index

Page numbers for photographs are in **boldface**.

belly, 16
biting, 14
body, 8, **9,** 20, **20**

coiling, 8, **9,** 21

eating, 4, **5**
eyes, 6, **7,** 20, **20**

hissing, 12, **13**

mouth, 4, **5, 13,** 20, **20**

predators, 12, 21

shedding, 10, **11,** 21
skin, 10, **11,** 20, **20**
sleeping, 6
slithering, 16, **17,** 21
smelling, 2
snakes, 3, 5, 7, 9, 11, 13, 15,
  17, 18, 19, 20

tasting, 2
teeth, 14, **15,** 20, **20**
tongue, 2, **3,** 20, **20**

underneath, 10, 21

About the Author

Apple Jordan has written many books for children, including a number of titles in the Bookworms series. She lives in upstate New York with her husband and two children.

With thanks to the Reading Consultants:

Nanci Vargas, Ed.D., is an Assistant Professor of Elementary Education at the University of Indianapolis.

Beth Walker Gambro is an Adjunct Professor at the University of St. Francis in Joliet, Illinois.

Library of Congress
Cataloging-in-Publication Data

Jordan, Apple.
Guess who bites / Apple Jordan.
p. cm. — (Bookworms: Guess who)
Includes index.
Summary: "Following a guessing game format, this book provides young readers with clues about a snake's physical characteristics, behaviors, and habitats, challenging readers to identify it"—Provided by publisher.
ISBN 978-1-60870-428-6
1. Snakes—Juvenile literature. I. Title.
QL666.06J67 2012
597.96--dc22   2011000329

Editor: Joy Bean
Publisher: Michelle Bisson
Art Director: Anahid Hamparian
Series Designer: Virginia Pope

Photo research by Tracey Engel

Cover: Xavier Eichaker/Peter Arnold/Photolibrary
Title page: Barry Mansell/Minden Pictures

The photographs in this book are used by permission and through the courtesy of: *Alamy*: avatar images, 3, 20 (top, left); Marcos Veiga, 7, 20 (middle, left); Susanne Masters, 17; *Animals Animals – Earth Scenes*: Peter Weimann, 5, 20 (top, right); *Getty Images*: Laura Wickenden, 9, 20 (middle, right); Theo Allofs, 13; Martyn Chillmaid, 19; *Corbis*: Joe McDonald, 11, 20 (bottom, left); *Minden Pictures*: Barry Mansell, 15, 20 (bottom, right).

Printed in Malaysia (T)
1 3 5 6 4 2